GOLF EPIDEMIC   LO LINKERT

ISBN 0-929097-02-5

LO-BOY GOLFTOONS NORTH AMERICA INC.
500 Capitol of Texas Hwy.
Building 3, Suite 200
Austin, Texas
78746

#1-8307 – 124th St.
Surrey, B.C., Canada
V3W 9G2

D1614299

GOLF EPIDEMIC

Golf is an incurable disease for which we hope they'll never find a cure! If you don't want to be infected by it, my advice is to never take a golf club in your hand and never never touch a golf ball. If you have, the bug has already got you. There is no escape! There will be no pain, just a steady itch and an irresistible urge to go out and hit the little ball with everything you've got. Naturally, the little white ball doesn't enjoy this too much so he plays little tricks on you by jumping off the tee right in the middle of your backswing or ducking as your club races at 100 mph towards him. If you take your eyes off him for just one moment, he makes you look like a fool. It is called a whiff and can be very expensive if you're a money player. It is very important when you catch the bug that you also give it to your other half, husband or wife. Otherwise you will see very little of each other (the couple that plays together, stays together).

This book will give you an inside look at what you'll face when you're infected by the disease called golf. It is the only disease in the world that will keep you healthy — physically, mentally and spiritually. It will enrich your life, give you many new friends and take your daily worries completely away. What are you waiting for?

OH MY GOD, YOU'RE CALLING YOURSELF A GOLFER ?!?

485 YDS
PAR 5

2

3

4

5

6

1

2

3

4

11

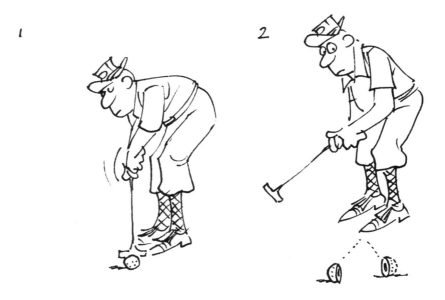

1   2

3

4

13

1

2

3

4

5

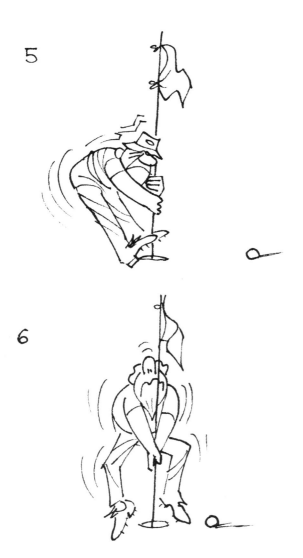

6

7

1

2

25

1

2

3

35

5

6

7

8

41

1

2

43

1

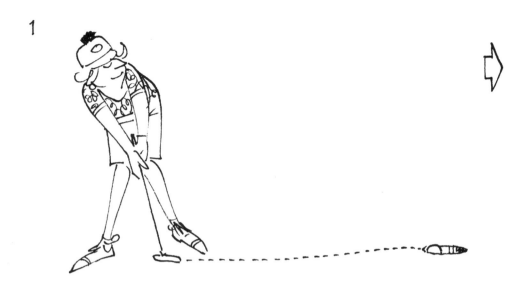

1

2

3

58

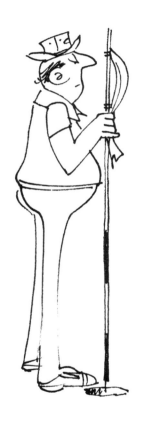

1

2

3

4

1

2

71

1

2

3

4

2

3

4

5

6

7

8

1

2

1

2

3

4

1

2

3

4

85

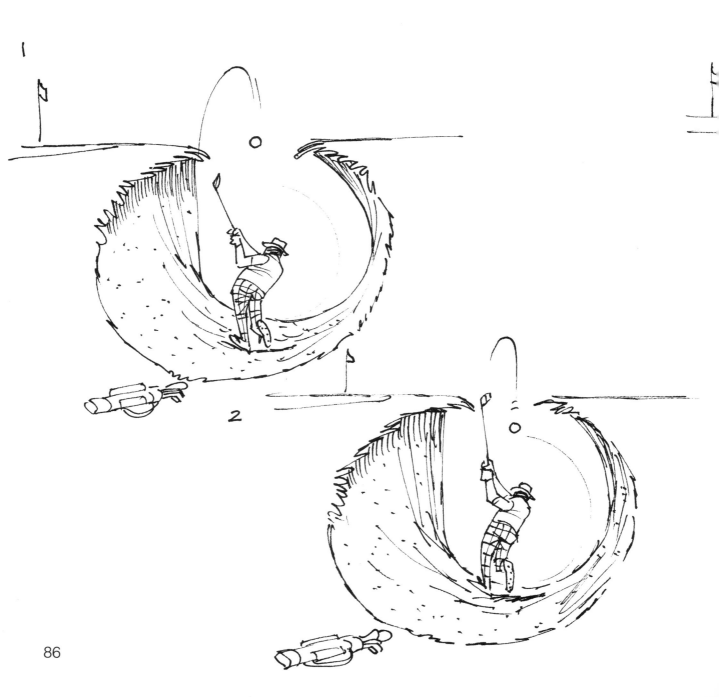

86

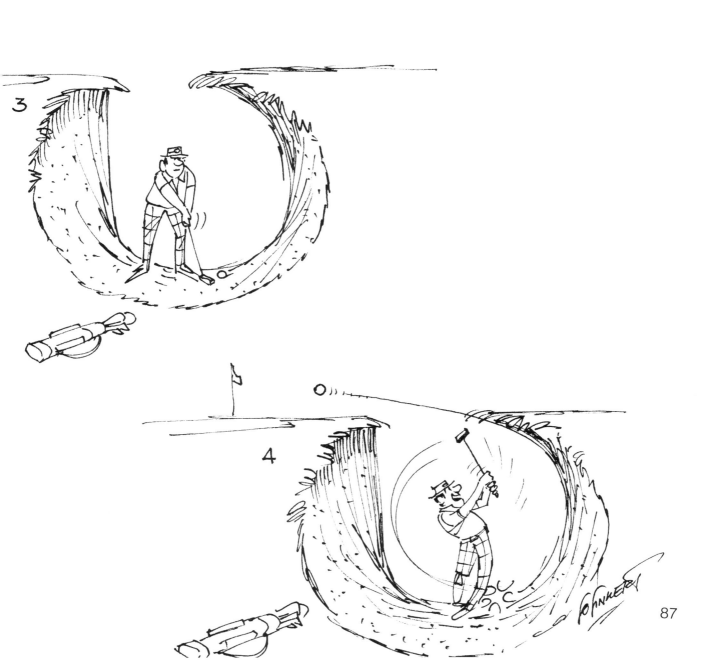

3

4

89

2

3

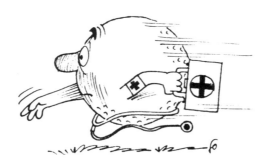

SCORECARD
SHREDDING
$1.00

If you take golfing too seriously, this book will change your outlook on golf! A perfect book for all occasions. Your golfing friends will love it. This book will make you "keep your head down".

'Dimples' the humanized golfball is Lo's creation and success story. A hilarious book about the long suffering golfball. All golfers will be able to sympathize with and relate to Dimples and his plight. Every golfer will enjoy this book - at the 19th hole, the locker room, or in the comfort of an easy chair by the fire.

Golf Calendars — in full colour. Each cartoon is vibrant and bright and suitable for framing. A sure hit for all golfing enthusiasts — to be enjoyed every day of the year.

Look for these items and other Lo-Boy Golftoon items in your favorite bookstore, pro shop or gift shop, or write to the publisher

LO-BOY GOLFTOONS OF NORTH AMERICA INC.
500 Capitol of Tx Hwy.
Building 3 - Suite 200
Austin, Texas
USA, 78746

IN CANADA:
#1-8307 - 124th Street
Surrey, British Columbia
Canada, V3W 9G2